Earth: Fast Changes

Table of Contents

by Erin Fry

Pictures To Think About i
Words To Think About iii
Introduction 2
Chapter 1 Earthquakes 4
Chapter 2 Volcanoes 14
Chapter 3 Storms 20
Conclusion 29
Glossary 31
Index 32

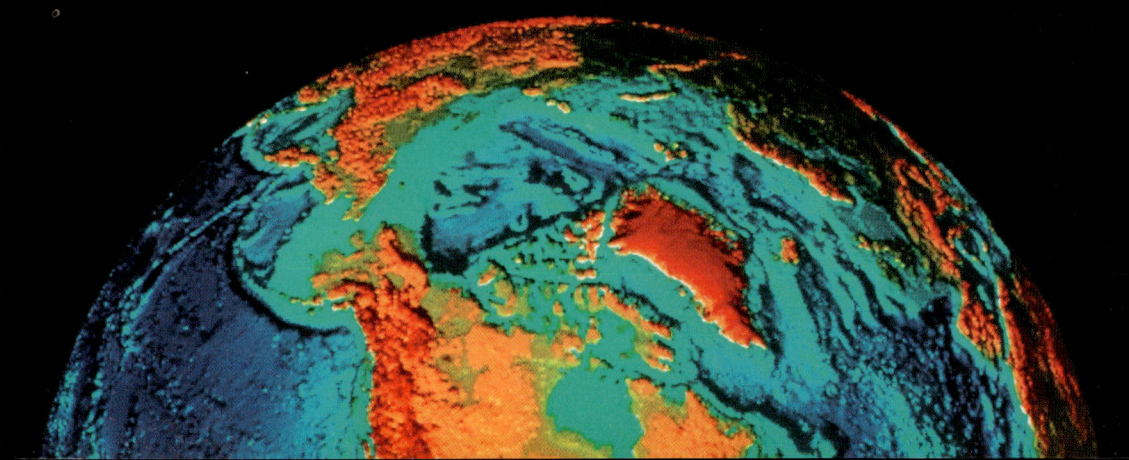

Pictures To Think About

Earth: Fast Changes

Words To Think About

plate

What do you think the word **plate** means in this book?

Meaning 1
a round, flat dish for food (noun)

Meaning 2
a thin, flat piece of metal (noun)

Meaning 3
a section of Earth's crust (noun)

eruption

What do you think the word **eruption** means?

Latin: *ex* (out)

Latin: *rumpere* (to break, rupture)

Read for More Clues

eruption,	page 2
magma,	page 14
plate,	page 5

magma

What do you think the word **magma** means?

- What is **magma**?
  - red-hot
  - ?
  - liquid
- Where can you find **magma**?
  - below Earth's crust
  - ?
  - inside volcanoes

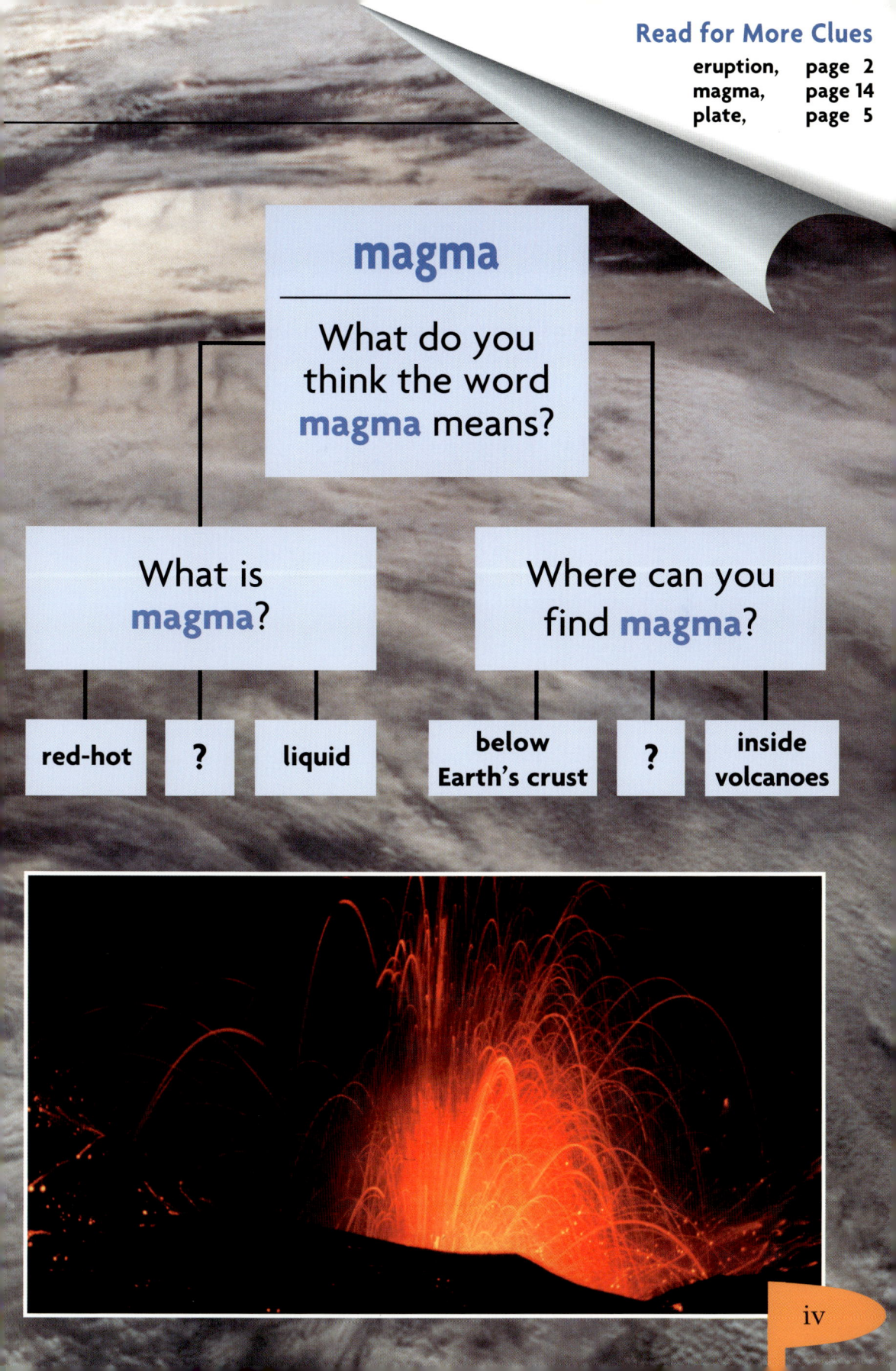

iv

Introduction

May 18, 1980. The sun is shining. The sky is clear. Then at 8:32 A.M., a **volcano** (vahl-KAY-noh) explodes. It **erupts** (ih-RUPTS). The **force** tears away one side of the mountain. Hot **lava** (LAH-vuh) shoots out. Snow and ice on the mountain melt away. Many animals die.

This is Mount St. Helens. Its eruption (ih-RUP-shun) was the biggest ever in the United States.

How can Earth change so quickly? Volcanoes are very powerful. **Earthquakes** (ERTH-kwakes) and big storms are also powerful. These things change Earth in just seconds. Read on to explore some of these fast changes.

▲ The surface of Earth is constantly changing shape. This is Mount St. Helens erupting in 1980.

CHAPTER 1

Earthquakes

It was early on an April morning in 1906. Most people in San Francisco were still asleep. Then a terrible earthquake hit the city. Many buildings fell down. Thousands of people died. The city burned for days.

▲ San Francisco in 1906, after the earthquake

Primary Source

The writer Jack London witnessed the 1906 San Francisco earthquake. This is what he wrote: "San Francisco is gone. Nothing remains of it but memories... great stores and newspaper buildings, the hotels and the palaces... are all gone."

Why Does Earth Quake?

Earth has many layers. The outer layer is the crust. The crust is the ground you are standing on. It is also the floor of the ocean.

The crust is broken up into huge pieces. The pieces are called **plates**. These plates move all the time. They float on the mantle (MAN-tul). The upper part of the mantle is hot, melted rock. Look at the diagram to see the layers.

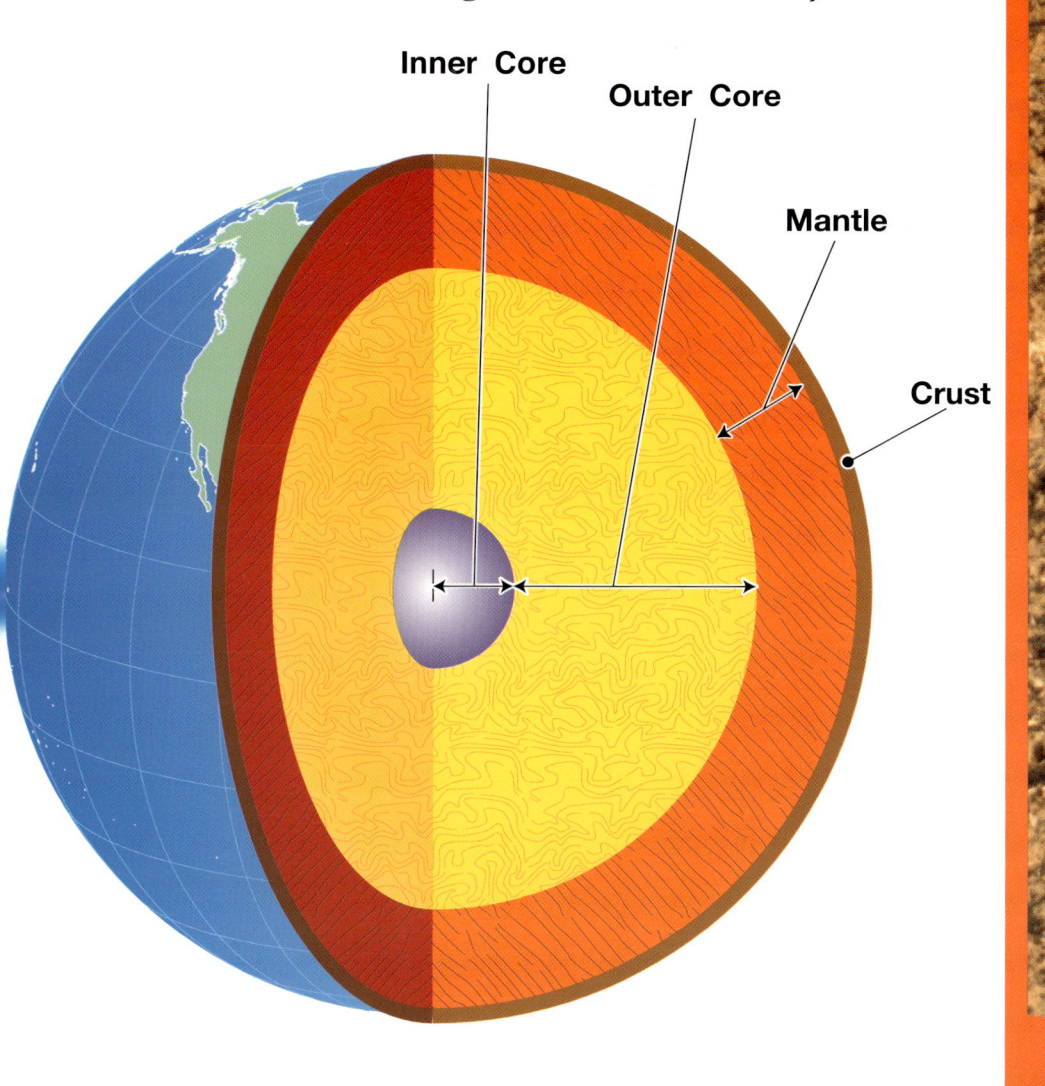

Inner Core
Outer Core
Mantle
Crust

CHAPTER 1

The crust has many cracks in it. These cracks, or breaks, are called **faults** (FAULTS). Sometimes rocks get stuck along a fault. The plates push hard against the rocks. If the rocks break, the plates move suddenly. This makes Earth's crust start to shake. This is an earthquake.

Scientists watch the large faults carefully. Earthquakes are likely to happen there again.

Types of Earthquakes

A. Blocks of rock move up or down along a crack.

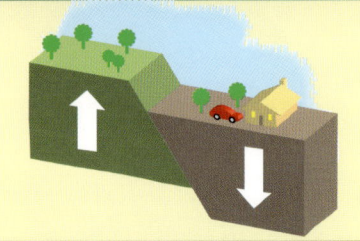

B. One block of rock slides up and over the other.

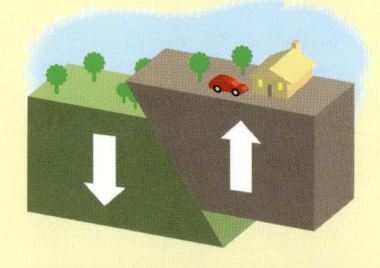

C. Rocks scrape sideways and sometimes up and down.

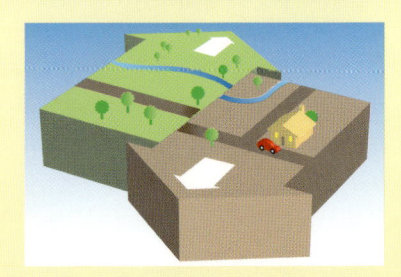

EARTHQUAKES

Earthquakes start underground. The point where an earthquake starts is called the focus. The epicenter (EH-pih-sen-ter) is the ground right over the focus. That is where the earthquake is its strongest.

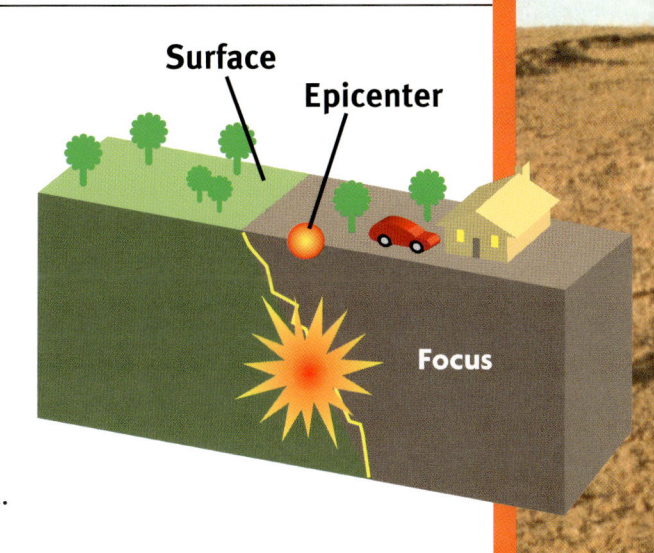

It's a Fact

Chinese Earthquake Predictor
The continent of Asia has the most earthquakes. Two thousand years ago, the Chinese people invented this tool to predict earthquakes. The dragons had little metal balls in their mouths. When an earthquake started, most people didn't feel it immediately. However, the little balls very noisily rolled out of the dragons' mouths and into the toads' mouths.

CHAPTER 1

Where Earth Changes

Earthquakes take place every day somewhere on Earth. Most earthquakes are small. They do little or no damage. The big ones can change the shape of the land.

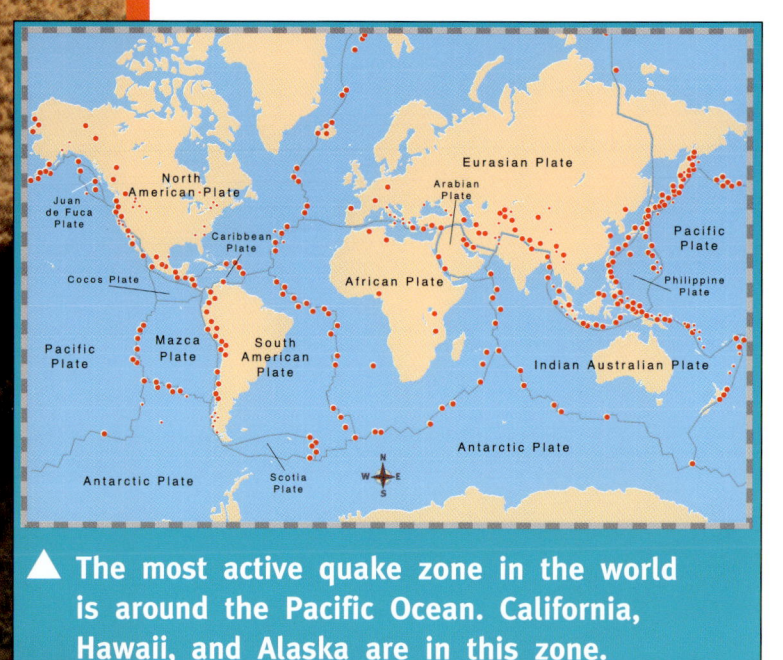

▲ The most active quake zone in the world is around the Pacific Ocean. California, Hawaii, and Alaska are in this zone.

They Made a Difference

Scientists use a seismograph (SIZE-muh-graf). This machine measures and records the strength of earthquakes from as far as 600 miles (966 kilometers) away! In 1935, Charles Richter (RIK-ter) invented a **scale**. The scale helped scientists read the seismograph more easily. Richter's scale goes from 1 to 9. It measures the **magnitude** (MAG-nih-tood), or power, of a quake. Each number is ten times stronger than the number below it. For example, a magnitude 4 earthquake shakes ten times more than a magnitude 3 quake. Earthquakes of 7 or above on this scale usually mean a lot of damage.

EARTHQUAKES

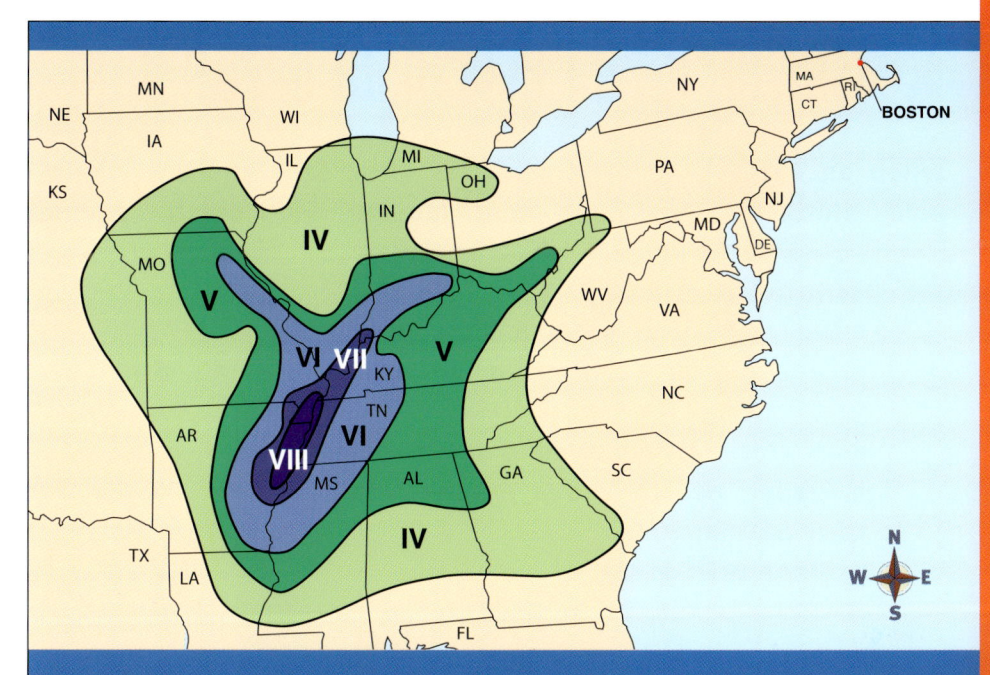

▲ The quake in New Madrid, Missouri, was felt at least 1,000 miles away in Boston, Massachusetts. Bells rang in church towers there!

Closer to Home

In 1811 and 1812, three very big earthquakes struck. The earthquakes took place near New Madrid, Missouri. They made big changes to the land.

Large areas of land sank. New lakes formed. Forests were destroyed. One quake even changed the path of the Mississippi River!

9

CHAPTER 1

Measuring the Effects of an Earthquake

When an earthquake happens, it is often felt far away. Does one place along the fault have more damage? Find out for yourself.

▶ ### What You Need
1. an empty box—like a shoe box.
2. about three tablespoons of lentils or small, dried beans
3. a ruler
4. a clock with a second hand, or a timer
5. paper, pencil, and a marker
6. a partner
7. floor with a rug

▶ ### What You Do
1. Make a chart to record what you see:

Place	Effects of Tapping the Box
Place 1 nearest the epicenter	
Place 2	
Place 3 farthest from the epicenter	

2. Place the box on a rug on the floor. Put a small handful of dried beans at each end of the box. Put a small handful of beans in the middle of the box.
3. Number the places 1, 2, and 3.
4. Hold the far end of the box firmly. Lightly tap on the other end. Keep tapping for 30 seconds.

10

EARTHQUAKES

5. Ask your partner to record on the chart what he or she sees in the box.
6. Switch places and do steps 2–5 again.
7. Compare what you saw.

If you are still curious about earthquakes, you might try to figure this out: If an earthquake lasts a short time, will its effects be different than one that lasts a long time?

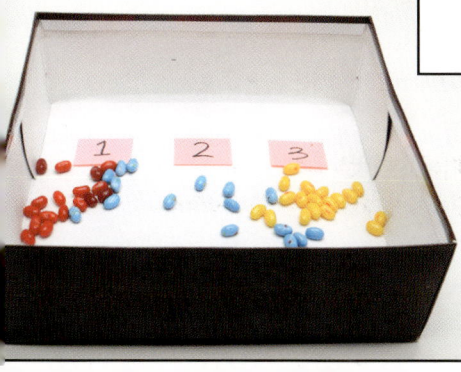

CHAPTER 1

The Tsunami of 2004

The date was December 26, 2004. It was a quiet morning in South Asia. Then an earthquake hit.

It struck deep in the Indian Ocean. The quake caused a **tsunami** (soo-NAH-mee), or giant wave.

The tsunami spread across the Indian Ocean. Its speed was 500 miles (805 kilometers) per hour! The wave slowed as it reached the shore. The wave also grew taller.

▲ Huge waves spread along the Indian Ocean and South China Sea. Waves spread to the coast of Africa. The waves covered small islands and moved tons of sand and earth. The land changed very quickly.

1. Solve This

A tsunami is traveling at a speed of 300 miles (482.7 kilometers) per hour. From a distance of 100 miles (160.9 kilometers) offshore, about how long will it take for the tsunami to hit land?

12

EARTHQUAKES

The people in South Asia had no warning. They saw the ocean do a strange thing. It pulled back suddenly. People could see the ocean floor. Fish flopped on the exposed ground.

Then a wall of water slammed onto the beach. The first wave was 30 feet (9.1 meters) tall. More than 200,000 people died. Houses were destroyed. Scientists are working hard to find a way to warn people next time.

▲ The tsunami in South Asia changed people's lives. In a matter of moments, it also changed the appearance of the land.

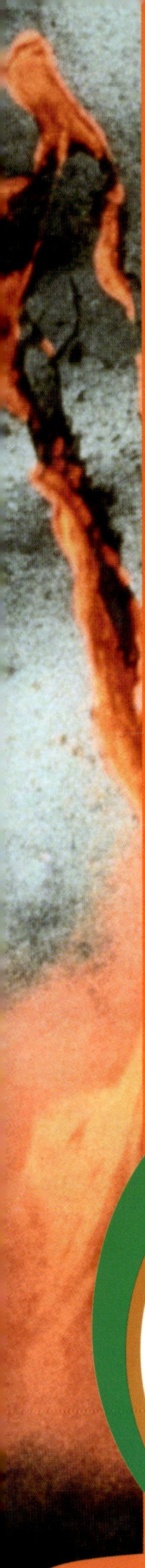

CHAPTER 2

Volcanoes

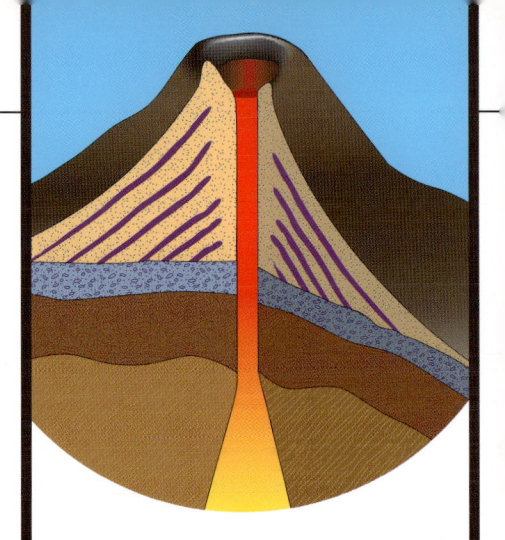

Mount Vesuvius is a famous volcano. This volcano is in Italy. It erupted in A.D. 79. A giant ash cloud rose 20 miles (32 kilometers) into the sky. Red-hot lava and rock, called **magma** (MAG-muh), rolled down its sides. The lava covered the old city of Pompeii.

Below Earth's crust, red-hot rock, called magma, rises up. Force from below pushes it up toward the surface. A volcano forms when magma and hot gases escape through openings in the surface of Earth.

It's a Fact

Ring of Fire

More than half of the world's volcanoes are located in what is known as the Ring of Fire. Most active volcanoes are in that zone.

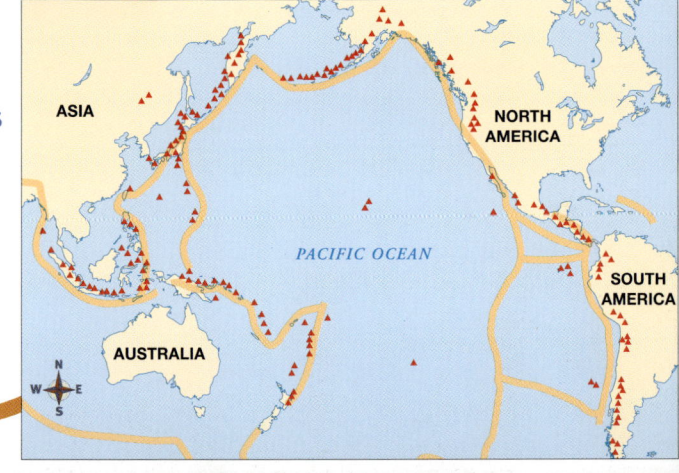

14

More About Mount Vesuvius

Vesuvius looks like a mountain. It has a cone at its top. This is where the ash, solid rock, and lava, or liquid rock, came blasting out.

This volcano has erupted many times. It has been quiet since 1944. People think it will erupt again in the future.

The First Volcanoes

Long ago, people thought volcanoes erupted because gods were angry with humans. The word *volcano* comes from Vulcan, the Roman god of fire.

▲ 1780 painting of Vesuvius erupting

15

CHAPTER 2

Careers in Science

Do you like to spend time outdoors? Are you curious about how Earth works? You might become a volcanologist (vahl-kuh-NAH-luh-jist). These scientists explore volcanoes all over the world. They study how and why volcanoes erupt. They also look for signs that might tell when a volcano is getting active. They study everything that comes out of a volcano and how Earth is affected.

VOLCANOES

New Islands

The ocean floor has many volcanoes. Seawater flows into the volcano's opening. The hot magma turns the seawater into steam. Then bubbles of steam burst through the ocean's surface. Over time, the magma can cool and harden. It builds up slowly. Sometimes it rises above the ocean. It forms new islands.

It's a Fact

Newest Island

In 1963, a volcano formed a new island off the coast of Iceland. The new island was named Surtsey (SERT-say). Seeds that traveled on the water or in the air took root on the island. Now, it is a nature preserve. People come to study what kinds of animals and plants grow there.

▲ the island of Surtsey being formed

▲ the island of Surtsey as it looks now

CHAPTER 2

Affecting the Weather and Earth

Volcanoes can change weather. An eruption can make heavy winds and rain in the area. Volcanic gases and dust can go around the world. This changes Earth's weather. The dust can hide the sun. Then Earth cools down.

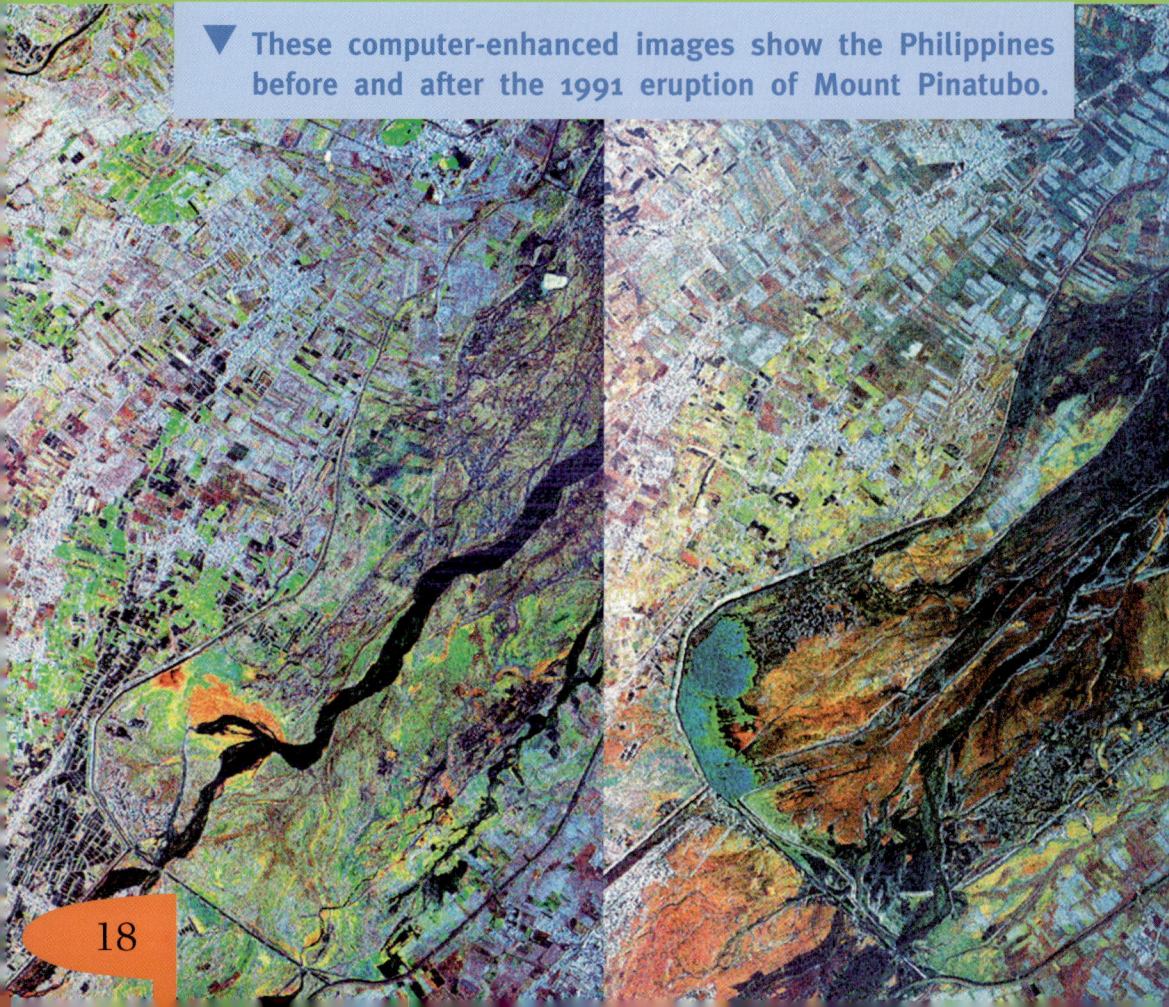

▼ These computer-enhanced images show the Philippines before and after the 1991 eruption of Mount Pinatubo.

18

VOLCANOES

▲ A volcano on Montserrat, an island in the Caribbean Sea, left the ash on this truck.

Some Good News

Ash and dust from a volcano can help the land. Ash and dust make soil good for growing crops. In East Africa, there is an active volcano called Karisimbi (kar-ih-SIM-bee). The soil around the volcano is very rich. Good crops grow there.

✓ Point   Make Connections

Read more about the 2004 tsunami at your school library or local library. Find out how people around the world have helped tsunami victims.

CHAPTER 3

Storms

A storm is headed to the coast! You turn on the TV. You want to see the weather report. The storm might get stronger. If it does, it will become a **hurricane** (HER-ih-kane).

▲ a NASA satellite photo of the eye of a hurricane

Hurricanes

Hurricanes start as small thunderstorms. Heat from warm ocean water speeds up the wind. The storm gets stronger.

The winds blow faster than 73 miles (117 kilometers) per hour. That makes the storm a hurricane. A hurricane can grow to be more than 100 miles (161 kilometers) wide.

2. Solve This

**A hurricane is 80 miles from land. The weather forecaster says it will hit land in 30 minutes. How fast is the hurricane traveling?
Answer in miles per hour.**

CHAPTER 3

A Hurricane Hits Land

A hurricane changes the land quickly. Strong winds knock huge trees down. Heavy rains wash away the soil that plants need to grow. High waves wash beaches away.

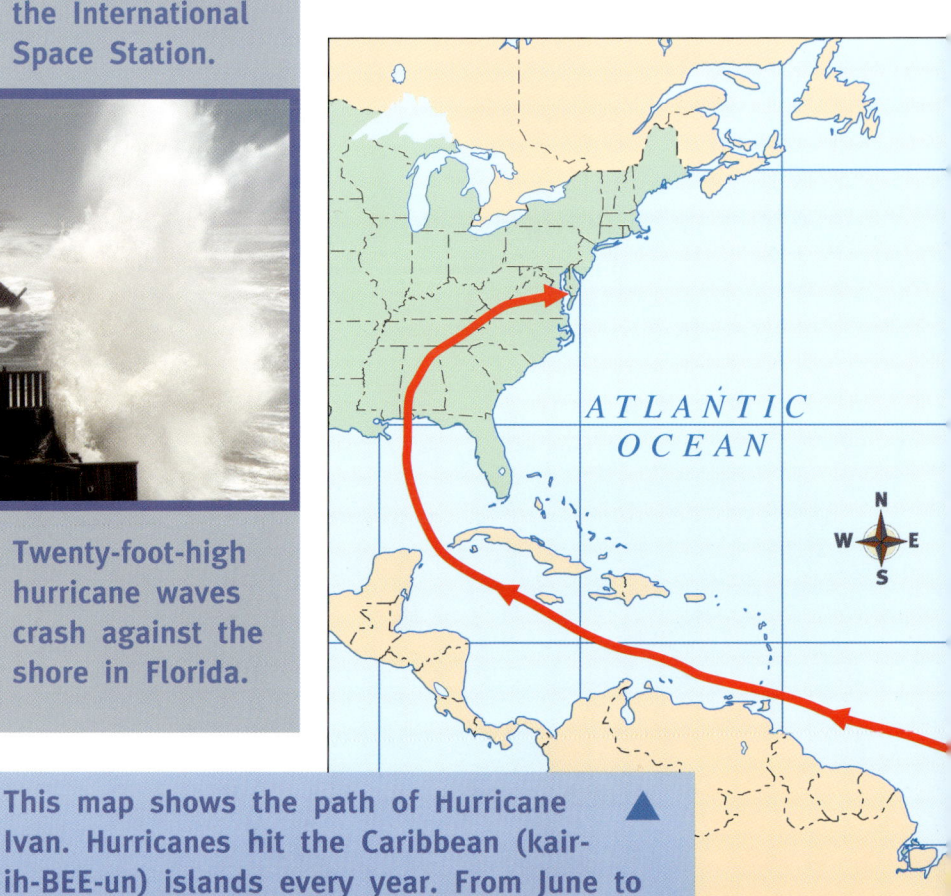

▲ This photo of Hurricane Ivan was taken from the International Space Station.

▲ Twenty-foot-high hurricane waves crash against the shore in Florida.

This map shows the path of Hurricane ▲ Ivan. Hurricanes hit the Caribbean (kair-ih-BEE-un) islands every year. From June to November, this part of the world stays ready.

22

STORMS

Storm Surges

Hurricane Ivan struck the coast of Alabama in 2004. Winds blew at 120 miles (192 kilometers) per hour. Heavy rains caused big floods.

The worst damage came from a **storm surge** (STORM SERJ). A storm surge is a rise in the level of the sea. It is caused by high winds.

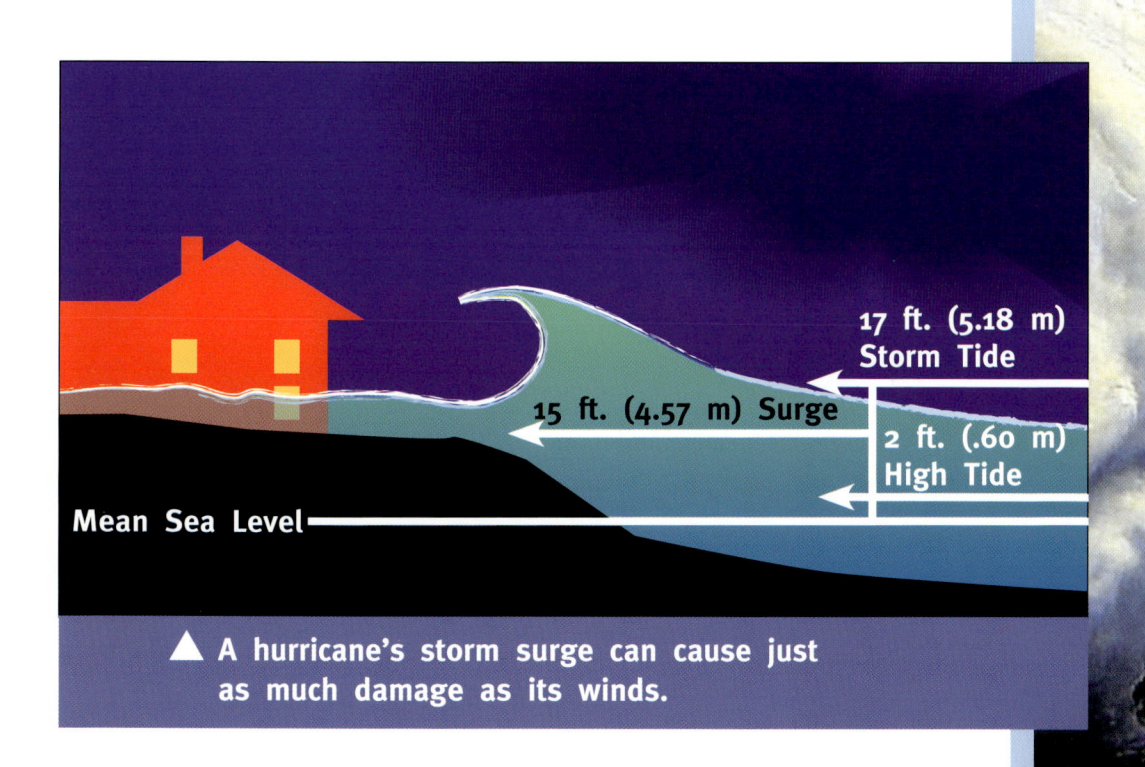

17 ft. (5.18 m) Storm Tide
15 ft. (4.57 m) Surge
2 ft. (.60 m) High Tide
Mean Sea Level

▲ A hurricane's storm surge can cause just as much damage as its winds.

CHAPTER 3

A storm surge can rise up to 26 feet (8 meters) high. Hurricane Ivan's storm surge was about 16 feet (4.9 meters) high. The tall waves changed the shape of the coast in two states.

It's a Fact

More than one hurricane can happen at the same time. And they move around a lot. Storm trackers needed a way to tell everyone which hurricane they were talking about. The problem was solved by naming them. Names of the worst hurricanes are never used again.

▲ This trailer park in Florida was completely wiped out in 2001 by Hurricane Andrew.

STORMS

Islands Get Smaller

Hurricanes can do great harm to islands. High winds and waves can wash away land. Some islands lose part of their beaches every year.

▲ This lighthouse had to be moved inland nearly 2,600 feet (792 meters) because the earth was beginning to wash away under it.

◀ Cape Hatteras, as seen from the space shuttle *Endeavour*

25

▲ the capital of Honduras after Hurricane Mitch

One Huge Change

Hurricanes bring heavy rain. The rain can carry away rocks and dirt. It can turn a hill to mud. The mud can slide down the hill suddenly.

In 1998, Hurricane Mitch hit Nicaragua (nih-kuh-RAH-gwuh). Heavy rain fell for days. Then a huge mudslide crashed down. Mud covered whole villages.

Everyday Science

The Power of Heavy Rain

Hurricanes aren't the only storms that can change Earth's surface. Sometimes, heavy rain is enough. Heavy rains are a common cause of mudslides. A whole hillside can begin to slide if it becomes very wet.

STORMS

Hurricanes Around the World

Hurricanes have other names. They can be called cyclones (SY-klonez). They can also be called typhoons (ty-FOONZ). The map below shows where these names are used.

The winds of a hurricane spin differently, too. South of the equator (ih-KWAY-ter), they spin clockwise. North of the equator, they spin the other way.

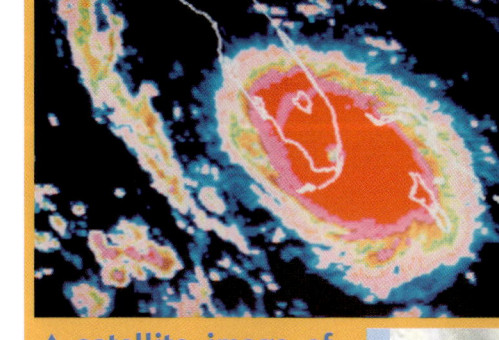

▲ satellite image of Hurricane Andrew

▼ People in certain parts of the world learn to get ready for the hurricane season. The map below shows you where most hurricanes take place.

Key
- Where hurricanes form
- Hurricane direction

27

CHAPTER 3

Monsoons

Every year starting in June, **monsoons** (mahn-SOONZ) bring four months of heavy rain to India. Monsoons are very powerful winds that change direction. They can cause flooding and landslides. Entire hillsides can be washed away after days of heavy rains. Flooding near river banks can destroy crops.

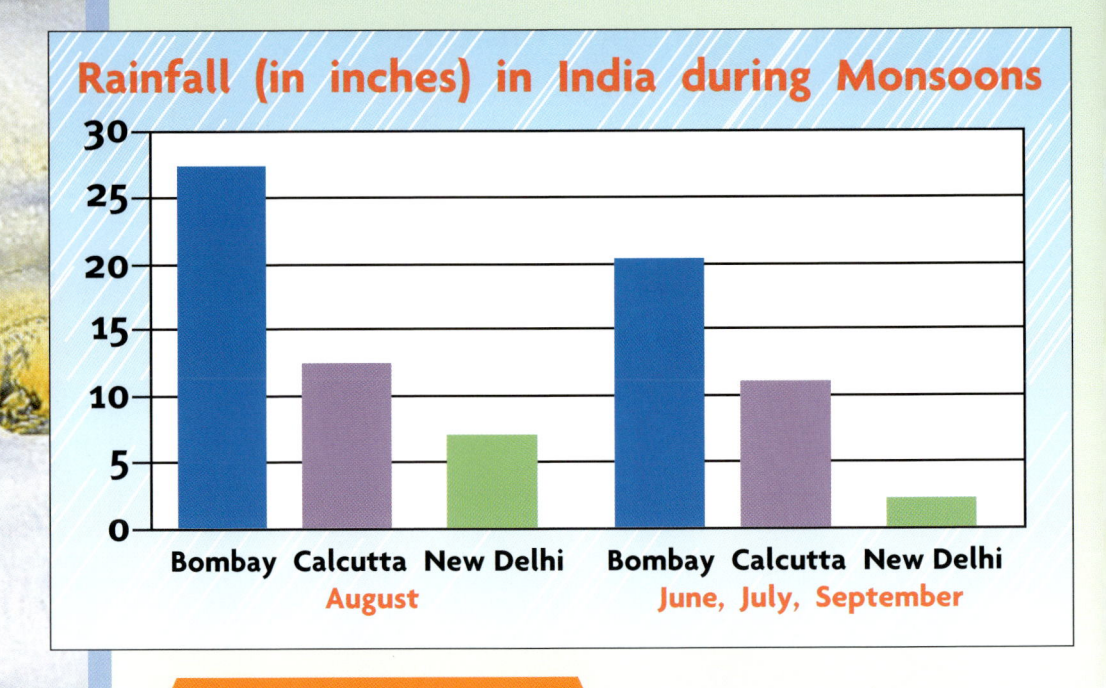

Rainfall (in inches) in India during Monsoons

City	August	June, July, September
Bombay	~27.5	~20.5
Calcutta	~12.5	~11
New Delhi	~7	~2.5

3. Solve This

Which city in India gets the most rain during the monsoon season? How many inches total does this city get in these four months?

✔ Point   Picture It

A wave taller than a house crashes onto the shore. Draw what this might look like. Be sure to show how a wave like this could change Earth's surface.

Conclusion

Earthquakes, volcanoes, and huge storms can change Earth. They can do it quickly. They can cause landslides, mudslides, and floods. Waves and winds can move rocks, dirt, and sand from one place to another.

Will those forces keep changing Earth? Yes, they will. We cannot stop Earth's changes. We can learn about them. We can find ways to reduce the harm they cause.

CONCLUSION

Talk It Over

Use the chart to help you summarize the three types of natural disasters. Name changes that all three of them can cause.

Disaster Effects

Earthquakes	Volcanoes	Hurricanes
faults, mudslides, rockslides, tsunamis; formation of lakes; forests destroyed	formation of islands, and others disappear; new craters; lava flows; forests destroyed	floods, forests destroyed; mudslides; land wears away

◀ The Oued Fodda (WED FOH-duh) Fault in Algeria (al-JEER-ee-uh) shows what the land looks like when one block of rock hangs over another one.

Glossary

earthquake (ERTH-kwake) shaking of Earth's crust (page 3)

erupt (ih-RUPT) burst out with great force (page 2)

fault (FAULT) a crack in the surface of Earth where rocks slide past each other during an earthquake (page 6)

force (FORS) a pushing or pulling action that can change the shape of something (page 2)

hurricane (HER-ih-kane) a large, powerful storm with high winds that forms over an ocean (page 20)

lava (LAH-vuh) red-hot, liquid rock that has reached Earth's surface from a volcano (page 2)

magma (MAG-muh) red-hot, liquid rock under Earth's crust (page 14)

magnitude (MAG-nih-tood) the size or power of something—in this case, the power of an earthquake (page 8)

monsoon (mahn-SOON) a strong, violent wind that brings heavy rains to parts of Asia (page 28)

plate (PLATE) a section of Earth's crust and upper mantle (page 5)

scale (SKALE) a system of numbers used to measure something, such as a ruler (page 8)

storm surge (STORM SERJ) a sudden rise in sea level caused by a storm (page 23)

tsunami (soo-NAH-mee) a large wave caused when an earthquake happens on the ocean floor (page 12)

volcano (vahl-KAY-noh) an opening in Earth's surface; a mountain that is formed from material that comes through this opening (page 2)

Index

earthquake, 3–13, 29–30
erupt, 2–3, 14–15, 18
fault, 6, 10, 30
force, 2–3, 14, 29
hurricane, 20–27, 30
Hurricane Andrew, 24, 27
Hurricane Ivan, 22–24
Hurricane Mitch, 26
landslide, 28–29
lava, 2, 15, 30
magma, 14, 17
magnitude, 8

mantle, 5
monsoon, 28
Mount Pinatubo, 18
mudslide, 26, 29
New Madrid, Missouri, 9
plate, 5–6
Richter, Charles, 8
Richter scale, 8
Ring of Fire, 14
scale, 8
seismograph, 8
storm surge, 23–24
Surtsey, 17
tsunami, 12-13, 19, 30
volcano, 2–3, 14–19, 29–30
volcanologist, 16

Solve This Answers

1. Page 12 20 minutes
If it takes one hour—60 minutes—to travel 300 miles, it would take 40 minutes to travel 200 miles. So it would take 20 minutes to travel 100 miles.

2. Page 21 It is traveling at 160 miles per hour. This problem has two parts.

A. You know that an hour has 60 minutes. You know that 30 minutes were spent traveling. The storm has thirty minutes (half of its hour) left to travel. 60 − 30 = 30 minutes.

B. The hurricane is at the halfway point: 80 miles from shore. You know that two halves make a whole. So: Multiply 80 x 2 = 160.

3. Page 28 Bombay. 48 inches
Compare the numbers on the graph. Bombay had the most rainfall. Add up the total rainfalls for Bombay.